one
frightened?

Aaaah!

Visit our website at www.skyponypress.com.

10 9 8 7 6 5 4 3 2 1

Manufactured in China, March 2024
This product conforms to CPSIA 2008

Library of Congress Cataloging-in-Publication Data is available on file.

Cover design by Elke Kohlmann & Kai Texel
Cover illustrations by Dagmar Geisler
US Edition edited by Nicole Frail

Print ISBN: 978-1-5107-7705-7
Ebook ISBN: 978-1-5107-7706-4

What Happens When I'm Scared?

How to Understand and Talk About Fear and Anxiety

Written and Illustrated by
Dagmar Geisler

Translated by Andy Jones Berasaluce

Sky Pony Press
New York

People get scared for all kinds of reasons.

Kim is afraid of the gray dog that belongs to the Köhlers.

Max is afraid of the dark.

Ollie fears that everyone will laugh at him.

Lottie is afraid of the older boys who always make fun of her.

Ms. Sebald is terrified of spiders.

Jasper is afraid of the creature under his bed. No one has ever seen it. Not even Jasper. "But it has to be pretty scary!" he says.

Riley is afraid that something bad will happen.

Cam gets scared whenever he's up very high.

Big strong Leo is afraid that Libby will say no when he asks her to marry him.

Uh...

Most of the time, we can sense when we're afraid.

We feel it in our bodies. And, because everyone is different, there are different ways to feel fear.

WHAT FEAR DOES TO US

It makes me weak at the knees . . .

My heart beats like crazy.

I have to suddenly use the bathroom.

I get goosebumps.

Goose-bumps, you say?

I feel like I'm running out of air.

I get really stiff and can barely move.

I have to cry sometimes.

Then this is me.

And me.

And that's me.

My hair stands up on end for hours. That's how it feels, anyway.

I get queasy.

I just want to run away.

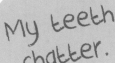

My hands get very sweaty . . .

My teeth chatter.

. . . and I get cold feet.

My stomach ties itself into knots.

I'm not afraid of of anything at all.

My breathing gets pretty fast.

I can't eat anything.

I can't think about anything else.

How do you experience fear?

These feelings are not that dumb. They actually help us pay attention. Fear exists to warn us of danger.

Our nerves sound the alarm:

It's important that we respond quickly, in the moment. The body reacts before we even think about it. Otherwise, we'd actually be too slow for some dangers.

After the initial fright, then other nerves start working for us.

This calms things down a bit, so we don't just go into a panic. All the abilities we have to help us avoid danger should work well. There's a lot going on internally when we're afraid. Many things can happen at the same time.

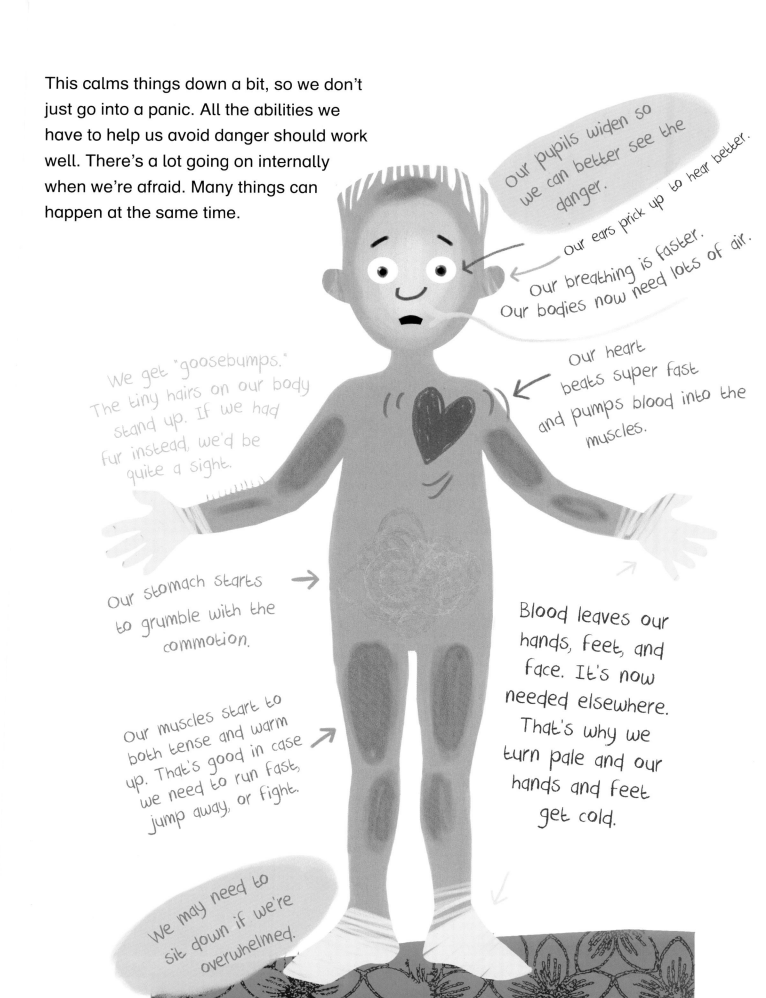

Fear is truly great. It watches over us and has us ready to go within seconds so that we can react to danger. And this program runs all by itself inside our bodies.

Nevertheless, it can be very taxing on the body. It takes strength and energy, even if we don't have to run away or scream or get help.

That's why, sometimes after an anxiety attack, a shock, or a fright, we may be quite weak and tired.

If the fear or anxiety lasts for a while, it's even more strenuous.

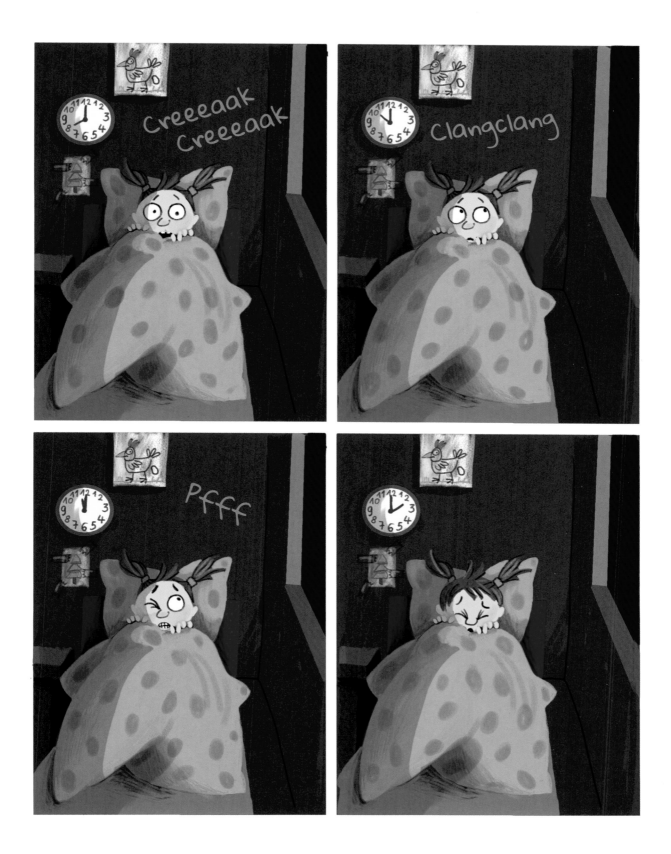

So, it's sometimes good to see for ourselves if what scares us is really something to fear.

That's easy: That's not its job. Fear has a lot to do so that we can get to safety in time. The rest is on us to do.

In the first moment of shock, it's good to act quickly. Thanks to fear, this often happens automatically. After that, there's usually enough time to think and ask yourself a few questions.

WHY AM

Am I afraid of something?

OR

Am I afraid of someone?

OR

Can I see it?
Can I hear it?
Can I smell it?
Is it here, near me?
Is it really there?
Do I need help?
Who can help me?

Who is it exactly?
Am I being threatened?
Am I being annoyed?
Am I being laughed at?
Do I need help?
Who can help me?

I AFRAID?

Am I afraid of doing something?

OR

Do I have no idea at all what I'm afraid of?

Is it dangerous?
Do I still need some practice?
Am I not doing it today because I'm too tired?
Am I afraid that someone will laugh at me?
Did someone tell me I can't do it, and do I just believe that?
Is it something I need to get a little bigger to be able to do?
Do I need help?
Who can help me?

Is the atmosphere here making me uneasy?
Am I sensing someone else's fear?
Have I ever experienced something that scared me, and is there something right now that reminds me of it?
Is someone trying to scare me?
Do I need help?
Who can help me?

If you deal with these questions, you'll get to the bottom of your fear. Sometimes that works fine. Namely, when there's a danger that's clearly recognizable. Or when you quickly realize that there's nothing to fear.

When the danger's over, the fear calms down, and so do you.

If you're afraid to do something, that fear goes away when you're sure you can do it. It even eases up once you dare to try something at least once.

You decide when you are ready. Nobody else can do that for you. Even if someone means well and says, "Don't be like that!" that doesn't make you feel any more ready.

But sometimes it's not quite that simple. The fear is there, and we struggle to figure out why.

Although Max gets scared as soon as it gets dark, he knows that the darkness can't harm him.

But then what's he afraid of? Max can't say for sure, especially not when he knows he's sitting in his room at home and it has just gotten dark.

When Riley fears that something bad might happen, she can't calm herself or her fears. Riley can imagine all the dangers vividly. She sees them in front of her, even when they're not there.

And it makes no difference when Mom and Dad say: "But it's all good. You're safe in your bed."

As soon as Mom and Dad are out of the room, fear sounds the alarm again, and Riley's heart beats in her throat. The whole fear program runs through her body. Over and over again. Sometimes it helps if Dad reads a funny bedtime story. Or when Mom comes to cuddle for a bit.

Some might think a fear like Riley's or Max's isn't that important. Or you could laugh at them both because they're afraid of something that's not actually there. But it's not that simple. You must always take fear seriously. It's a feeling, and a feeling shows us that something's happening inside us. This also applies when we can't see exactly what that is.

Halima has fears similar to Riley's. She has trouble falling asleep at night because of her fear. She often wakes up at night and screams because she has bad dreams. Halima comes from a country at war. What she experienced there frightened her so much that she can no longer remember it. That sometimes is the case when something bad has happened.

Since then, Halima's fear has been all over the place. She can't calm down, even though everything is peaceful around her now.

Riley, luckily, has never experienced anything so bad. But she's a sensitive child who takes everything very much to heart. Also, she has a big imagination, so she can picture everything very well. Even things she only casually picked up from hearing bits of news reports.

Max is afraid of the dark because he once saw a scary "grown-ups only" movie. And Jasper has just as much imagination as Riley. He believes that there's a nasty creature under his bed, although anyone has yet to see it.

Such feelings of fear are very exhausting, because they keep coming and just don't stop.

And that's not how it should be! Riley and Mom had an idea. Riley drew her fear on a piece of paper, and then she and Mom made the creature that emerged out of wool. Now Riley can speak to her fear.

We're going over here. It's safe. You'll really enjoy the view.

Jasper didn't talk to his fear, but he and Dad did talk to the critter under his bed. No one has seen it yet. And it's still nasty, Jasper thinks, but not to him. It promised to only be nasty if someone came along who wasn't nice to Jasper. Since then, Jasper has been able to sleep well and so has his fear.

Nobody has to be alone with their fear. It's good to talk about it with someone you trust.

Cam gets an idea from his brother to talk his fear into being on good terms with him. Fear likes this. Then it doesn't have to exert itself so much and can rest a little until it might be needed again.

But sometimes you need help. Halima now speaks to a woman who is very knowledgeable about feelings. She's a therapist. Halima can talk to her about her bad dreams, and very slowly, step by step, they get Halima's fear back on track. Every so often, they manage to calm the stirred-up fear a bit more.

If fear could talk, it would also have a few tips.

Try not to listen when someone laughs at you because of me. It's not nice of them, anyway!

Sleep well! Eat healthy things! Go out often into the fresh air! If you're in shape, I don't have to hustle as much.

Talk to others about it if you are afraid, no matter what it is. Even though there are two of us (you and me), it's sometimes not enough.

Be safe. You already know: buckle up, helmet, kneepads, lifejacket. . . . I won't act out so much if you follow this advice when trying something new.

A few rules, because rules keep us safe. For example: Don't go with strangers or wander off with anyone your parents have told you to avoid. Make a checklist just in case you get lost. Follow traffic rules. Get help if you find anything strange or scary.

Be brave when it makes sense for you to be brave. And don't let anyone tell you you're a coward if you don't feel up to something.

Don't feed me stuff that's too scary. Especially nothing only intended for adults. Otherwise, I'll wear myself out at some point, or I'll totally freak out. Neither reaction will help you one bit.

Confide in someone if you keep feeling me. That will do you good.

Don't let anyone scare you. You don't need more fear. You have me. If anyone tries, get help.

Have fun with friends and laugh a lot. That strengthens the soul.

It's true: fear doesn't like being overfed spooky stuff. But what it does like is when you tickle it a little with a suspenseful story or a game, for example. It enjoys that—and maybe you do, too.

And at any time, you can say: "That's enough!"

fear is our friend.

If it takes care of us and we take care of it, together we can experience a lot. And that's very nice!

Advice and Help

"Anxiety," Child Mind Institute, https://childmind.org/topics/anxiety/

"Anxiety in Children," Anxiety Canada, https://www.anxietycanada.com/learn-about-anxiety/anxiety-in-children/

"A Child Therapist's Favorite Resources for Calming Anxiety in Children," Coping Skills for Kids, https://copingskillsforkids.com/calming-anxiety

"Childhood Fears and Worries," Nemours KidsHealth,, https://kidshealth.org/en/parents/anxiety.html

"Child Psychologist's Favorite Resources for Parents and Kids for Anxiety," Child Guidance Resource Centers, https://cgrc.org/blog/child-psychologists-favorite-resources-for-parents-and-kids-for-anxiety/

"Normal Anxiety," Worry Wise Kids.org, https://www.worrywisekids.org/node/70

Afterword

Why am I so afraid?
That's a good question.

And when we know what the reason is for our fear, it's easy to answer. Fear is our warning system. It draws attention to danger, so we can react and get help. So, it's as simple as that?

No, it's not always that easy.

Fear is a strong emotion, and it can really get to us. "Nothing's as bad as the fear of it," my mother used to say when I was a child. Because I was a bit like Riley in this book. I could vividly imagine all the dangers, and with my overactive imagination, I pictured a lot of additional horrible things.

As a child, you often cannot tell whether a danger is real or only imagined. Even adults find it difficult at times. Like everything, the threat may not always be real, but the fear is, so it takes action in our bodies and comes with unpleasant consequences. It wants to be taken seriously. Taking it seriously doesn't mean, however, that we add fuel to the fire. It is this differentiation that matters to me.

Fear is an important part of our psyche. The goal is not to get along without it, but to learn to live well with it.

That's something people can practice, and as with many other topics, it helps to talk to one another. This book can be a reason for conversation.

Dagmar Geisler

© Jahreiss.com

Dagmar Geisler has already supported several generations of parents in accompanying their children through emotionally difficult situations. With her Safe Child, Happy Parent picture book series, the author and illustrator sensitively deals with the most important issues related to growing up, from body awareness to the exploration of your own emotional world to social interaction. Her works always include a helping of humor, especially so when the matter is serious. Her books have been translated into twenty languages and have been published in the United States and elsewhere.

Shiver
Shiver

Is any

here